What Happens When You Die . . . For Real!

What Happens When You Die . . . For Real!

Whatever It Is – Make Sure You Have Your Affairs in Order

Leneiva Head

Clovercroft Publishing

What Happens When You Die…for Real!

Published by Clovercroft Publishing, Franklin, Tennessee

Author photos by Bobby Quillard

Edited by Ann Tatlock

Cover and Interior Design by Suzanne Lawing

Printed in the United States of America

ISBN: 978-1-968127-21-3

Contents

Foreword

I wrote this book because too many people avoid one of the most important topics in life—what happens when it ends. We don't talk about wills, power of attorney, or final wishes until we're forced to. And by then, it's usually too late.

As a real estate broker, I've had the honor of helping many families navigate moments when it's time to move —some joyful, and others deeply painful. Time after time, I found myself working with clients who were completely overwhelmed after the loss of someone they loved.

I've worked with a lot of seniors. I've learned that many of them want to get things in order, but they don't always know how. Some are afraid to face it. Others don't know who to trust. Many are living on a fixed income and believe planning is out of reach.

The final story was almost always the same: someone either ran out of time before putting plans in place, or they made plans but never shared them. Either way, the burden fell to the family—and too often, they were left to figure it out on their own.

What's worse, I witnessed how quickly the very idea of "family" could unravel under that kind of pressure. Grief, frustration, and confusion don't always bring people together. Sometimes, they drive a wedge between even the closest relatives. I saw siblings stop speaking, cousins cut ties, and parents and children fall into silence. It all could have been prevented—if only someone had taken the time to prepare and communicate.

That's why this book exists.

I want to help people understand—truly understand—what happens when you die. Not just in a legal sense, but in a practical, emotional, and spiritual one. My hope is that this knowledge stirs something in you. I hope that it inspires you to extend mercy to those you love by planning ahead. To have those hard conversations now, so your family doesn't have to fight their way through uncertainty and pain later. Families should draw closer to one another during loss—not fall apart.

So I wrote this book to meet people where they are. Whether you're a parent trying to protect your children, an adult child navigating a loved one's affairs, or a senior who just wants peace of mind—I see you. I wrote this to help you get started. Because starting is often the hardest part.

Inside, you'll find explanations, templates, and stories that make something that seems so complex feel a little simpler and doable. You don't have to know everything. You just have to begin.

And now, you have a place to begin.

— *Leneiva Head*

Chapter 1:

It Happens

This is not another book about life after death. Death. I know it is a dark subject. One that no one likes to talk about until it's too late. Of course, the day it becomes too late, is too late. I do not want you to read this book and think dark thoughts. It is not designed for that. It is designed to encourage you to think about giving. It's designed to encourage you to think about those you love. It's designed to encourage you to think about what you can do differently to help those you may leave behind.

As you continue reading, I encourage you to laugh when you find yourself relating to some of the crazy stories I share. It is my hope that those same stories will inspire you to act. Don't worry, this book is designed to show you how not to put those you love through what happens when you die … for real.

Are you part of a family that has the same answer for all of your "let's plan for the inevitable" questions? You know, the dreaded "do you have a will" question? Often followed by two dreaded responses. Response number one: "We don't talk about stuff like that." Response number two: "Why? Do you think I have some money or something?" HA! I'm sorry, I had to laugh with you on that one because I know you can relate.

The reality is, we don't want to think about it, much less talk about it. Keep reading to find out what could happen if we don't. As you read, think about the one funeral home you wouldn't be caught dead at. Do you have one in mind? Good. Follow me.

A young man barely thirty years of age was living with his girlfriend. He became very ill.

No one talked to him about the importance of life insurance or saving for the future. After all, he was barely thirty! He did not survive his illness. His family had to make the final arrangements.

Remember the funeral home you wouldn't be caught dead at? That's the funeral home that handled this young man's final arrangements.

There was no life insurance or savings account funds to apply to the cost of the final arrangements. Why else would anyone choose that funeral home? They suggested a graveside service. It was free. You had to be on time and the service could last no more than fifteen minutes. No big deal, right? Keep reading.

Have you heard the phrase: You'll be late for your own funeral? This young man actually was. That's right, the funeral home got him to the cemetery 45 minutes late! You should've seen it! Picture the hearse pulling into the cemetery on two wheels going about 60 miles per hour on that one-lane dirt/gravel road that leads to the grave site … kicking up dust and rocks all along the way! Unbelievable, right? Keep reading.

During the ceremony, the funeral home representative and his sidekick struggled to do the eulogy. A dead give-away was the fact that the funeral director kept calling the deceased man Antonio. His name was Anthony. Interestingly, if you looked six inches to the funeral director's right, you'd see the name Anthony inscribed on the temporary marker. Can you believe it?!

During the closing prayer, not only did the funeral director's assistant receive a phone call, but he also actually answered the phone! HA! Yes, that's me laughing with you again.

Amazing!

To add insult to injury, a nervous bystander accidentally hit the panic button on his car. Yes, the car alarm chirped for five minutes. Yes, five minutes! Are you picturing this?

Did you know that only about 50% of Americans have life insurance? Of that, 42% know they don't have enough insurance coverage![i] This is the part where I ask you a question. Do you have life insurance? If not, do you have enough money saved to cover the expenses for your final arrangements? This will prevent your loved ones from having to call that last funeral director on the planet, knowing they're truly the worst funeral home on the planet.

Have you ever been asked to donate to the funeral fundraiser? You know, where a key family member begins calling the rest of the family asking for donations. Have you ever received the sad story accompanied by the infamous link to GoFundMe, CashApp, Zelle … you get the point? Think about it. What else can you do but make the donation? I've been asked to pay the grave opening fee. At the time the fee was $1,500. Now that was a hard pill to swallow. What would you have done? Talk about being put on the spot. I don't think there's a spot any bigger than the funeral fundraiser!

I know that you have someone that you love dearly. Would you want them to endure the missteps that Anthony's family endured? I know you wouldn't want anyone to spend time

setting up the funeral fundraiser! We can laugh now. I'm certain it was not funny at the time. You and your family deserve much more than a comedy of errors for lack of options. Would you agree?

If you answered no to my question earlier—you know, the one about whether you have life insurance—don't worry. This book is filled with information and tools designed to help you put a plan in place.

Chapter 2:

So, Plan Ahead

People say it's never too late to start planning. The truth is, when you're gone – it's too late.

You know how it goes because you've either experienced it or know someone who has. Experienced what? The family argument about the funeral arrangements. It starts with who will pick up the body and it's downhill from there. Conversations about who the better funeral home is will soon turn into arguments about who knows whom and who can give a better discount for services. Then comes the question about insurance. Was there an insurance policy? How much was it? Who's the beneficiary? This becomes speculation about how much money will be spent on the funeral arrangements versus how much money the beneficiaries will try to keep for personal use. Will they decide to have you cremated to keep more money for themselves? Will they skimp on the cars the family should ride in to the funeral and only get one, knowing that one car won't hold the entire family? A flurry of calls between various family members begin – all negative, of course. No one will confront the beneficiaries of the insurance policy. They'll just speculate among themselves. It's quite a spectacle!

Would you believe that after meeting with the funeral home, making funeral arrangements, and ordering one car instead of two, more drama occurs? Yes, the almighty program must be arranged. This sparks a new flurry of calls and speculation. Who will sing? How many solos will there be? Is Mother Johnson available to read the acknowledgements because that's what she always does? Which church should host the service? Who should do the eulogy?

I've walked out on a eulogy before. That guy didn't even know my uncle, but there he was talking a bunch of nothing as if he knew everything. It was a total travesty. I managed to endure my aunt's eulogy because at least that preacher asked me about her the night before the funeral.

That way he could pretend as though he knew her well. That went over like a lead balloon! I kid you not. It was all I could do to remain seated.

This is why it is so important to plan ahead. I know it may seem difficult to do. You will indeed have to rise to the occasion. Decisions need to be made. Cemetery, crematorium, mausoleum? Where do you want to be? Did you know you could rent a casket for the sake of your loved ones saying goodbye one last time, then be cremated afterward? I know, I know … more than you'd like to think about … yet very necessary just the same.

Take some time to find the funeral home of your choice. They will help you put together your final arrangements. Did you know that you can pay for your final arrangements in installments? What I think you'll find helpful is knowing that some memorial facilities have a network of locations so if you put together a plan in one city or state and relocate more than 75 miles, your plan relocates with you! Some facilities also provide bereavement travel assistance, making it easier for out-of-town family members and friends to attend. How amazing would it be to allow your loved one to simply make a phone call and know that everything is already in place? If you've not yet experienced it, writing an obituary is a horrible process. Selecting caskets and floral arrangements is gut wrenching. Being gouged by the funeral home is the worst. You can save your loved ones from this level of pain. Allow them to simply celebrate the life they enjoyed with you! You've given them various gifts all along the way during life. Give them this one. It will be well worth it.

Write your own obituary, select your own final outfit or at least the colors, select your final resting place, and a casket. FYI … If you don't select your own casket, you may be subject to the whims of a disgruntled family member. Someone who may order a different casket than originally selected with the family - on the day before family visitation and viewing. Oh no! You'll be forced to miss your own visitation/viewing – because the new casket will not be ready for another week! Yes, this happened … for real! Select your own flowers, write your eulogy, and select the officiant (preferably someone who actually knows you). Be sure to select the right amount of family cars for the funeral. Plan to allow time too for loved ones to attend the repast and still have transportation back home. If not, this could happen to your loved ones:

True story!! The homegoing celebration for a very important man lasted for what seemed like forever. His widow was elderly and very kind. The service lasted so long, it crept into her mealtime. To keep her blood sugar from dropping, there was a race (during the service) to find snacks. After rushing to the car and finding peanut butter crackers in the console, a friend shared them with her. It was a good thing too, because they hadn't begun reading the acknowledgements and resolutions yet. Who knew it'd last a grueling 45 minutes?! It was so bad that after 20 minutes, each time the lady opened her mouth and said, "We the members of the church of … do hereby resolve and acknowledge," everyone in the sanctuary literally groaned out loud. Imagine that! After the service was finally over, or so I thought, I witnessed the most unusual thing – a casket drive-by! Yes! A casket drive-by. Typically, after the service, the officiants roll the casket out to the hearse and the family walks out behind the casket. Imagine my amazement when I saw the casket being rolled out or, so I thought, only to watch them roll it in front of the family on the front row from left to right and back – like an old typewriter carriage moving side to side!! This was how they handled the final goodbye part of the service. They rolled the casket and, just like doing the wave at a football game, when the casket passed by, folks would fall out, vomit, or scream hysterically. Then the casket came back and the same wave of activity would reoccur—fall out, vomit, scream hysterically. This happened four times!

Naturally, sometime during the repast, the limousine driver said he had to leave because his time was up. Those who had ridden in the family car had left their personal belongings in it.

Imagine discovering that not only is the family car gone, requiring you to find a way home, but your coveted Louis Vuitton shoes are still in that car! Would it be too much stress on your funny bone to tell you that they also left the widow's wheelchair on the sidewalk?! As a result, those who rode in the family car were left scrambling to find a way home. As for the wheelchair, it was left on the sidewalk because no one had room in their car or truck for it. Luckily, it was still there waiting for a ride later that night.

I will warn you, however, that with all this planning, devious behavior may still occur. I'm not sure how to tell you to plan for the dissemination of bad information. Yes, there has been a time when a certain family member deliberately gave someone the wrong service time.

Apparently, there was no love lost for that family member. The service was at noon. They were given a time of two o'clock. I don't have to tell you they missed the funeral! For real!

SAMPLE OF THINGS TO DO WHEN PLANNING FINAL ARRANGEMENTS

1. Select a Funeral Director

1. *Research Funeral Directors:*
    - Look for funeral homes in your preferred area. SAC: What requirements should the place have?
    - Visit their websites and/or request brochures and service details. SAC: What details should I ask about? See Questions to Ask section.
    - Ask for referrals from friends/family.
2. *Set up a Consultation:*
    - Ask about package options for burial and cremation.
    - Request an itemized list of costs. SAC: What are some of the itemized costs and what should I beware of that may not be needed?
3. *Reputation*:
    - Check reviews online (Google, Yelp, or funeral-specific directories).
    - What do your friends and family say about the company?

2. Decide on Burial or Cremation

1. *Burial*:
   - More traditional.
   - Involves selecting a casket, cemetery plot, and grave marker.
2. *Cremation*:
   - Flexible (ashes can be kept, scattered, or buried).
   - Generally less expensive.

3. Find a Resting Place (Mausoleum or Ground Burial)

1. *Mausoleum*:
   - Can be indoors or outdoors.
   - Ideal for above-ground preferences. SAC: What about laws the govern burials, such as in New Orleans they are mostly above ground.
   - More costly than a ground burial.
2. *Ground Burial:*
   - You'll have to choose a cemetery plot.
   - A headstone or grave marker is an additional expense.
3. *For Cremation:*
   - Columbarium (niche for urn storage).
   - Take home.

- Scatter ashes at a special location.

4. Select an Officiant

1. *Religious Leader:*
   - Contact the spiritual leader of your faith.
   - They often customize services.
2. *Secular Officiant:*
   - Seek an officiant for non-religious ceremonies.
3. *Family Member/Friend:*
   - Consider someone close to you for a more personal touch.

5. Budget

1. *Get Quotes For:*
   - Funeral home services.
   - Cemetery or crematorium fees.
   - Transportation and other services.
2. *Consider Prepaid Plans:*
   - Some funeral homes offer payment plans or discounts for prearranged services.

6. Design Your Final Outfit

- Design your look. What do you want to wear? What color do you prefer?
- Do you want to include accessories?

- Be mindful that some traditions may require specific attire.

7. Flowers or Donations

1. *Flowers*:
    - Choose arrangements (wreaths, sprays, casket flowers).
    - Work with a florist to select colors or themes.
2. *Donation*:
    - In lieu of flowers, suggest an important cause that people can support.

8. Music

- Select hymns, classical pieces, or meaningful modern songs.
- Hire musicians or singers for a live performance.
- Use recorded tracks with a quality sound system.
- Match music to eulogies, reflections, or the procession.

9. Program

Think about:

- Opening words, music, eulogy, readings, closing remarks.

- Include photos, quotes, and personal touches.
- Decide on printed and/or digital programs.

10. Where Will Service Take Place

- Funeral home, church, outdoors, chapel, community hall, private location.
- Location for Repast if applicable.

SAMPLE OF THINGS TO THINK ABOUT WHEN SELECTING A CASKET

1. What's It Made of:

- *Metal*:
  - Common types: steel, stainless steel, copper, bronze.
  - Steel is available in different gauges (thickness levels).
- *Wood*:
  - Options include pine, mahogany, cherry, walnut, or oak.
  - Wood caskets often have a classic, traditional appearance.
- *Alternative Materials:*
  - Biodegradable caskets for green burials.
  - Cardboard or wicker for simpler, eco-friendly options.

2. Understand Metal Gauge Numbers:

- Gauge number refers to the thickness of the metal.
- A lower gauge number means the metal is thicker and more durable.
  - 16-gauge: Thickest most durable.

- 18-gauge: Commonly used, slightly thinner than 16-gauge.
- 20-gauge: Most cost effective, thinner than 18-gauge.

- Copper and bronze are measured in ounces per square foot (e.g., 32 oz., 48 oz.).

3. Sealed or Not Sealed:

- Sealed (gasketed): Designed to resist water and air entry.
- Non-sealed (non-gasketed): More affordable.

Did You Know:

Under the Federal Trade Commission's (FTC) "Funeral Rule," you are not required to purchase a casket from the funeral home.

- **Comparison Shop:**
    1. *Costco / Sam's Club:* Offer quality caskets at lower prices delivered directly to the funeral home.
    2. *Online Retailers:* Provides options and delivers directly to the funeral home.
    3. *Local Suppliers:* Some communities have local craftsmen or businesses that make custom caskets.

4. *Funeral Home:* Often more expensive.

Request a "General Price List" from the funeral home to see their options without pressure.

The content provided is for informational purposes only and should not be considered legal advice. For personalized assistance or verification of legal compliance in your jurisdiction, consult with an attorney or estate planning professional.

SAMPLE QUESTIONS TO ASK THE FUNERAL DIRECTOR

General Services:

1. *What are your available service packages?*
   - Ask for details on what's included in each package (e.g., viewing, embalming, transportation).

2. *Can you explain the burial and cremation options?*
   - Clarify the differences, costs, and processes for each option.

Costs:

3. *What is your General Price List?*
   - This itemized list will help you understand all the fees and services available.

4. *Are there any additional fees not listed in the General Price List?*
   - Confirm there won't be surprise charges.

Casket and Merchandise:

5. *Do I have to buy a casket from you?*
   - The answer should be no; it's your right to purchase from another provider.

6. *What are the price ranges for your caskets, urns, or burial vaults?*

Preparation of the Deceased:

7. *Do I need embalming?*
    - Embalming is often not required by law, especially for direct burial or cremation.

8. *What are the options for dressing and presenting the deceased?*
    - Discuss preferences for clothing and any personal touches.

Cemetery and Burial:

9. *Can you help with selecting a cemetery or mausoleum?*
    - Ask if they coordinate with local cemeteries.

10. *Do you handle the burial vault, headstone, or grave marker arrangements?*
    - Some services may not include this.

Cremation:

11. *Is cremation done on-site or through a third party?*
    - If outsourced, inquire about the process and oversight.

12. *What are the options for the ashes (urns, scattering, columbarium, etc.)?*

Customization and Personalization:

13. *Can the service be personalized?*
    - Ask about the ability to use photos, videos, music, or themes.

14. *Can family members or friends participate in the service?*
    - Some may wish to speak, sing, or contribute in other ways.

Legal and Administrative:

15. *How many certified copies of the death certificate will be provided?*
    - Most families need several copies for legal and financial purposes.
16. *Can you assist with Social Security, Veterans' benefits, or life insurance claims?*

Additional Services:

17. *Do you offer grief counseling or referrals to support groups?*
18. *Are transportation services (e.g., hearse, limousine) included in the package?*
19. *Ensure all costs are disclosed upfront.*

SAMPLE FUNERAL HOME PRE-PLANNING AGREEMENT

Pre-Planning Agreement The Funeral Home
123 Anywhere St, Anywhere, IL 12345
(555) 123-4567
Pre-Planning Document for: John Johnson Date: January 1, 2020

1. Personal Information

Full Name: John Johnson Date of Birth: April 1, 1969
Place of Birth: Anywhere, Illinois
Social Security Number: [XXX-XX-XXXX]
Next of Kin: Jane Johnson (Daughter)
Contact Information: (555) 234-5678
janejohson@janejohnson.com

2. Funeral Service Arrangements

- Type of Service: Traditional Funeral with Burial
- Visitation/Viewing:
  - Location: The Funeral Home
  - Date: Unknown
  - Time: 12pm-2pm
- Funeral Ceremony:
  - Location: The Church

- Date: Unknown
- Time: 12:00 PM

- Graveside Service:
    - Location: The Memorial Park
    - Date: Immediately following the ceremony

3. Disposition Arrangements

- Type: Burial
- Cemetery: The Memorial Park
- Plot Details: Section A, Plot 22
- Headstone Inscription: "Love You Eternally."

4. Merchandise Selected

- Casket: 18-gauge steel, gun metal gray with ivory interior ($2,500).
- Outer Burial Vault: ($1,200).
- Clothing: Dark Gray suit. Gray/White pin-striped dress shirt, dark gray necktie.
- Flowers:
    - Casket Spray: Red and White Roses, Baby's Breath, Carnations ($500).
    - Standing Spray: 3 - White Roses with Sash "Eternal Love" ($600 total).

5. Music and Personalization

- Music Selections:
  - Prelude: "Going Up Yonder" (Piano)
  - Reflection: "Jesus" by Josh Groban
  - Exit: "Take Me to the King"
- Photo Slideshow: 40 photos to be provided

6. Financial Details

- Total Cost: $9,900
- Payment Plan: Prepaid in full through a funeral trust account.
- Service Includes:
  - Basic Services of Funeral Director and Staff: $2,500
  - Embalming and Preparation: $1,150
  - Use of Facilities for Viewing: $500
  - Transportation (Hearse & One Limousine): $550
  - Graveside Service Coordination: $400

7. Additional Preferences

- Charity Donations in Lieu of Flowers: The Charity Organization.
- Total Copies of Death Certificate: 10
- Obituary Placement: The Newspaper

8. Emergency Contact for Changes

- Name: Jane Johnson (Daughter)
- Phone: (555) 234-5678

Agreement Confirmation

I, John Johnson, have reviewed and approved the above pre-planning selections. I understand that I may make changes to these arrangements.

Signature:________________________________

Date: January 1, 2020

Funeral Director's Signature: _________________

Date: January 1, 2020

The content provided is for informational purposes only and should not be considered legal advice. For personalized assistance or verification of legal compliance in your jurisdiction, consult with an attorney or estate planning professional.

Chapter 3:

Because Where There's a Will...

Where there's a will, there's a way! People say that all the time. In this situation, they couldn't be more correct. Did you know that while more than 50% of Americans believe having a will and estate planning documents is important, only 24% actually have them?![ii] Would you believe the main reason is procrastination? This is according to Caring.Com's 2025 Will and Living Trust Survey. Think about it at your next social function. For every 10 people in the room, only 2 may have taken the time to prepare a will. With a will in place, things will go a lot smoother for your loved ones should you leave them behind someday.

I'll never forget the day I decided to have a will drawn up. I thought it'd be relatively easy. Then I spoke to an attorney. So much for that concept. Why?

you ask. Because I had to think about the people I was willing to trust with certain aspects of my life while living and after I'm gone. Then, I had to think about who'd be willing and able to do so. Who was bold enough to stand up to certain members of my family in the event they disagreed with an act or decision being carried out on my behalf? Who wouldn't wipe me out if I had to give them Power of Attorney in the event I could not act or make decisions for myself for specific reasons? How long did I want to remain on life support? What kind of life support was I willing to be placed on, if at all? Did I want to be an organ donor?

To answer these questions, I had to have conversations with the people who I believed would have my back no matter what. I was forced to have the conversation that no one wants to have. Do you know what their response was? "I need to do my will too!" Well, alrighty then! Let's do it!

You see there's more to having a will prepared than simply addressing the division of your assets. Your attorney will ensure that you include a Health Care Directive which has instructions for your health care decisions should you become unable to make such decisions for yourself.

This is also known as a Living Will or Advanced Care Plan. The attorney will also ensure that you have a Durable Power of Attorney in place. This allows someone to handle your affairs for you should you become incapable of doing so. Please heed my warning: Don't bestow the honor of handling your affairs on someone who is always in need. You will soon realize that the money you had set aside for your well-planned homegoing celebration is gone.

I must say after I finalized my will and left the attorney's office, I felt accomplished and a bit strange. I had just made decisions about what should happen when I die. It was just weird, but necessary. Take some time out, contact your attorney or estate planner and get the ball rolling. Allow me to share a few stories of what could happen if you don't.

A young lady's aunt passed away after a long-term illness. She had a key to her aunt's home, so after leaving the hospital, she decided to stop by and check on things. There were cars parked in the driveway and in the grass! It looked a lot like a yard sale. She didn't need to use her key because the doors were unlocked and wide open. People were walking out of the house carrying things they had decided they were entitled to. They had practically taken everything that was in the home. She stopped one of her cousins and asked where he was going with those blankets. The cousin responded, "I know Auntie would've wanted me to have these." I don't have to tell you that an argument broke out, then there was a lot of yelling, a lot of cursing, people were thrown out of the house, and some have not spoken to each other to this day. For this reason, some people make it clear that their home should be locked up until their will has been read. I think this is a very wise decision.

When people don't think you have a will, they tend to do some pretty strange things. Much like the strangers who show up at the family reunion claiming to be Cousin Pete from your mom's side twice removed, children that no one knew you had show up and lay claim to a portion of your estate, sparking controversy from here to eternity and possibly dividing your family. There's a great sentence that your attorney can add to your will to curtail random claims against your estate: Those not named herein were intentionally excluded. Boom!

Here's food for thought. What will happen to your children if you don't leave instructions? Do you really want to leave this decision up to the state? Don't assume that your family will step in. Have the conversation, get an understanding, and include the instructions in your will. Trust me, if the state decides for you, your children will have to pay for your failure to plan.

True story: After my friend's wife died, her brother waited for my friend to leave the room, then he called the Social Security Administration and posed as my friend. He wanted to redirect the Social Security Benefits designated for my friend and his children such that the funds would be sent to him instead of my friend. It almost worked too! He had given the Social Security Administration his address in another state, the deceased wife's information (all of which he knew since he was her brother), and the children's names! They asked for the Social Security number about the same time that my friend re-entered the room and like an idiot, he handed the phone to my friend. When my friend got on the phone, the woman on the line stated that she needed to verify specific information before she could complete the process for Social Security benefit distribution. My friend elected to tell her that he had not initiated the call and would manage the process in person. True story!! To drive this point home, everyone has a will. The difference is whether it's the will you draft, or the will the state drafts for you. Which would you prefer? For real!

SAMPLE CHECKLIST FOR ESTATE PLANNING

1. Organize Personal and Financial Information

- Personal Details:
    - Full legal name, date of birth, and Social Security number
    - Current address and contact information
    - Marital status and family information (spouse, children, dependents)
- Financial Information:
    - List of bank accounts (checking, savings, certificates of deposit)
    - Investment accounts (stocks, bonds, mutual funds)
    - Retirement accounts (IRAs, 401(k) s, pensions)
    - Business ownership details (if applicable)

2. List Assets and Liabilities

- Assets:
    - Real estate properties (home, rental, vacation properties)
    - Personal property (vehicles, jewelry, collectibles, electronics)

- Life insurance policies
- Intellectual property or royalties

- Liabilities:
  - Mortgages
  - Auto loans
  - Credit card debts
  - Medical or other outstanding bills

3. Create or Update Legal Documents

- Will:
  - Appoint an executor to manage your estate.
  - Specify how assets should be distributed to heirs or beneficiaries.
  - Name a guardian for minor children (if applicable).
- Living Will/Advance Directive:
  - Specify your healthcare wishes in case of incapacity.
  - Include decisions regarding life support, organ donation, etc.
- Power of Attorney:
  - Financial Power of Attorney: Designate someone to handle financial matters.
  - Healthcare Power of Attorney: Designate someone to make medical decisions.

4. Plan for Minor Children or Dependents

- Appoint a legal guardian in your will.
- Set up a trust to manage inheritance until they reach adulthood.
- Ensure adequate life insurance coverage for their needs.

5. Review Beneficiary Designations

- Check and update beneficiaries on:
  - Life insurance policies
  - Retirement accounts (IRAs, 401(k) s)
  - Payable-on-death (POD) or Transfer-on-Death (TOD) accounts
- Ensure consistency with your will or trust.

6. Establish Trusts (if applicable)

- Revocable Living Trust:
  - Avoid probate by transferring assets into the trust.
  - Maintain control of assets during your lifetime.
- Irrevocable Trust:
  - Protect assets from creditors or reduce estate taxes.
- Special Needs Trust:

- Provide for dependents with disabilities without jeopardizing government benefits.

7. Plan for Taxes

- Review federal and state estate tax exemptions and liabilities.
- Strategize charitable giving to reduce taxable estate value.
- Consider gifting assets during your lifetime (up to the annual gift tax exclusion).

8. Secure Digital Assets

- Create a list of online accounts (banking, email, social media, subscriptions).
- Provide login credentials in a secure, accessible location.
- Specify how digital assets should be managed or deleted.

9. Communicate Your Plan

- Share your estate plan with key individuals (executor, power of attorney, guardian).
- Provide access to essential documents or let them know where they are stored.

10. Store Documents Securely

- Keep originals in a fireproof, waterproof safe or secure online storage such as a digital vault.
- Provide copies to your attorney or trusted individuals.
- Include:
    - Will and trusts
    - Power of attorney forms
    - Advance directives
    - Insurance policies
    - Deeds and titles

11. Periodically Review and Update

- Review the estate plan every 2–3 years or after major life events:
    - Marriage, divorce, or remarriage
    - Birth or adoption of a child
    - Death of a family member or beneficiary
    - Significant changes in assets or laws

12. Seek Professional Assistance

- Consult with:
    - An estate planning attorney
    - A financial advisor
    - A tax professional
- Ensure all documents comply with state laws and reflect your wishes accurately.

13. Prepare for Final Arrangements

- Write a letter of instruction for:
    - Funeral and burial or cremation preferences
    - Contact information for family, friends, and professionals (attorney, CPA)
    - Location of documents and safe deposit boxes Optional: Download and Use Estate Planning Templates Consider templates for:

- Wills
- Power of attorney
- Trust agreements
- Asset inventory forms

The content provided is for informational purposes only and should not be considered legal advice. For personalized assistance or verification of legal compliance in your jurisdiction, consult with an attorney or estate planning professional.

SAMPLE QUESTIONS TO ASK WHEN CHOOSING AN ESTATE PLANNING ATTORNEY

Expertise and Experience

1. What is your primary area of practice?
2. How many years of experience do you have in estate planning?
3. How many estate plans have you completed?

Services Offered

6. What estate planning services do you provide?
7. Can you help with tax planning or strategies to minimize estate taxes?
8. Do you assist with probate and trust administration?
9. Do you handle digital assets as part of the estate plan?
10. Can you help me set up a trust for minor children or dependents?

Fees

11. Is there an initial consultation fee?
12. Do you offer a menu of services?

13. What is your service rate?
14. What is your service rate for updating/revising estate planning documents?

Expectations

15. What do I need to do to prepare for our first meeting?
16. How do you ensure my estate plan remains up to date?
19. How will we communicate throughout the process?
20. Will I be working directly with you or your staff?

Special Considerations

22. Do you have experience with blended families or second marriages?
23. Can you help with charitable giving or setting up a charitable trust?
24. Do you have experience with business succession planning?
25. Can you work with my financial advisor or accountant?

References and Reputation

26. Can you provide references from past clients?
27. Do you have reviews or ratings online?

28. Are you a member of any estate planning organizations?
29. Have you been involved in any disciplinary actions?

The content provided is for informational purposes only and should not be considered legal advice. For personalized assistance or verification of legal compliance in your jurisdiction, consult with an attorney or estate planning professional.

Chapter 4:

They Say Sharing Is Caring

So, you've purchased a life insurance policy and even had your estate planning documents drafted. Now what? Share, share, share! There's nothing worse than knowing that your family member had a will, yet you're unable to prove it. How many times have you heard the question after losing a loved one: Did he/she have a will? What answer do you hear? Yes, I'm sure he/she did. Where is it? Who knows! Now everyone is in a panic because they don't know where to find the will and without it, they can't prove that there was a will. What about an insurance policy? How will we pay to bury him/her? Now I know he/she had an insurance policy. Where is it? Who was the insurance company? Oh boy … another dilemma.

I know you're craving another amazing story. Have I got one to share! An older gentleman passed away. He was a prominent figure in town. He even had a will. He also had a wife with a friend who was a notary. You can probably already guess where this is going but I absolutely must continue. That's right, his wife and her friend who was a notary fabricated a second will. Yes, it is forgery! Yes, it is illegal! Yes, they not only did it, but they also tried to pass it off as the official will. They even used it during a casual reading of the will. You didn't think the story ended there, did you? That would be too easy. Imagine how the rest of the meeting went when the original will was produced during the reading of the fraudulent will. There was a bit of back-room discussion that involved offers of reporting the notary to the authorities and possible incarceration. He confessed and the reading of the will was carried out using the correct version. I know it sounds unbelievable but, believe me, you can't make this stuff up! The family's saving grace was that this gentleman was wise enough to have shared his will with others, leaving no room for doubt as to what his final wishes were. Because a lot of people don't share, the wife and the notary assumed they could easily get away with it. I guess they learned what happens when you assume. I am often amazed at the lengths people will go to when you die … for real!

Don't stop at sharing the fact that you have insurance, a will, or other estate planning documents in place. Share the fact that you have a Health Care

Directive and what your end-of- life wishes are. Are you an organ donor? Do you have certain feelings about life support? How much support will you accept? Do you want life support at all? According to The Conversation Project National Survey 2018, while 92% of Americans think it's important to discuss their end- of-life care wishes, only 32% had actually done so.[iii] Surprisingly, that number has gone down 10% to a measly 22% as of 2023, according to Hospice News. iv I've peppered this book with comedic stories too absurd to be anything but hilarious; however, it's difficult to find any humor in the handling of someone's final stage of life. It is simply a harrowing, stressful, frightening, gut-wrenching process to go through as the next of kin with no instructions. When do you say no more?

No more:

- Watching your loved one suffer.
- Debating with family members on what's the best decision.
- Meeting with the doctors and counselors in the private family room having discussions about what is currently happening to your loved one internally.
- Questioning what to expect next, how soon to expect it, and whether or not your loved one is in pain.

- Wondering what happens if/when you make the ultimate decision.

This is probably not what you want your loved ones to go through. Losing someone you love is very hard. Being the one responsible for making the decision whether to discontinue life support is terrifying. It is a memory that never leaves you. I know because I counseled my aunt during the process of making this very decision for her husband of more than 50 years, my very dear uncle. The one question she continued to ask me was, "What should I do?" The two questions she continued to ask the doctors were, "Will he be in pain? Will he feel anything?" I stayed with him and comforted him until he took his last breath. Will your loved ones be forced to ask these same questions? Is this the turmoil you want your family to experience when they could simply follow your instructions? Does it make the outcome easier? Of course not! Does it help knowing that you made the decision for yourself versus forcing them to do it for you? It absolutely does.

At some point, you may have been privy to end-of-life conversations and the flurry of opinions and accusations that fill the room, all aimed at the next of kin forced to make a final decision on someone else's behalf. It's not an event worthy of envy. If you've never witnessed this feat, consider yourself fortunate … for real!

SAMPLE TEMPLATE FOR ORGANIZING YOUR FINAL AFFAIRS

1. Details

- Full Name: ______________________________
- Date of Birth: ______________________________
- Social Security Number: ______________________
- Address: ______________________________
- Phone Number: ___________________________
- Email Address: ___________________________
- Marital Status: ___________________________
- Spouse/Partner Name: ______________________
- Children/Dependents (Names & Contact Info):

  ____
- Pets (Type & Care Instructions):

  ____

2. Emergency Contacts

1. Name: ___________________________

   Relationship: ______________________

   Phone Number: _____________________
2. Name: ___________________________

Relationship: ______________________________

Phone Number: ____________________________

3. Medical Information

- Primary Care Physician: ______________________

  Phone Number: ________________________________

- Health Insurance Provider: ____________________

  Policy Number: ________________________________

- Medications: _____________________________________

- Allergies: ____

4. Final Arrangements

- Funeral Home Preference: _______________________

  Contact Info: __________________________________

- Burial or Cremation: _____________________________

- Burial Plot or Urn Location: ____________________

- Religious or Cultural Requests: _________________

  Prepaid Funeral Plan? [] Yes [] No

  Plan Details: __________________________________

- Obituary Wishes: _________________________________

5. Accounts

- Bank Accounts:

  1. Bank Name: ____________________________

Account Type: ______________________________

Account Number: ___________________________

2. Bank Name: _____________________________

Account Type: _____________________________

Account Number: ___________________________

- Retirement Accounts (401k, IRA, etc.):

3. Institution: _______________________________

Account Number: ___________________________

4. Institution: ______________________________

Account Number: ___________________________

- Investments (Stocks, Bonds, Mutual Funds, CD's):

5. Institution: _______________________________

Account Number: ___________________________

Expiration Date: ____________________________

6. Insurance Policies

- Life Insurance Provider: ___________________________

  Policy Number: ___________________________________

- Health Insurance Provider: _________________________

  Policy Number: ___________________________________

- Home/Auto Insurance Provider: ____________________

  Policy Number: ________________________________

7. Documents

- Will or Trust Location: ____________________

  Executor/Trustee Name: ____________________

  Contact Info: ____________________

- Power of Attorney Location: ____________________

  POA Holder Name: ____________________

  Contact Info: ____________________

- Safe Deposit Box Location and Box Number:

  ____

  Key Location: ____________________

- Deed/Property Titles Location: ____________________

8. Debts and Liabilities

- Credit Cards:

  1. Card Issuer: ____________________

     Account Number: ____________________

  2. Card Issuer: ____________________

     Account Number: ____________________

- Loans (Mortgage, Auto, etc.):

  3. Loan Type: ____________________

     Lender Name: ____________________

     Account Number: ____________________

9. Digital Accounts

- Email Accounts:

    1. Provider: ______________________________

       Username: ______________________________

       Password: ______________________________

- Social Media:

    2. Platform: ______________________________

       Username: ______________________________

       Password: ______________________________

- Online Subscriptions:

    3. Service: ______________________________

       Username: ______________________________

       Password: ______________________________

10. Additional Notes

- Special Instructions or Requests:

____

Be sure to keep this in a safe place, let your loved ones know where to find it, and keep the information current.

The content provided is for informational purposes only and should not be considered legal advice. For personalized assistance or verification of legal compliance in your jurisdiction, consult with an attorney or estate planning professional.

Chapter 5:

Sometimes It's Complicated

This is a special chapter dedicated to Veterans. Let me first simply say to the Veteran who's reading this: Thank you for your service and your sacrifice!

As a Veteran, you have a few more things to consider when preparing information to share with your family. I know you know where your discharge papers are (DD-214), but do your loved ones? Please make sure your loved ones have a copy or know where and what it is. Why does this matter? Because the Department of Veteran's Affairs asks for information like name, Social Security number, date of birth, and date of death. Your loved ones will surely know that information. But will they know the following: military service number, service entry date, service entry location, service exit date, service exit location, and any wars you may have fought in? Did you receive any medals or awards? Share these details!

So far, I'm probably not telling you anything you don't already know – but your loved ones need to know too.

The number of VA forms that your loved ones will have to fill out is maddening! The information on your (DD-214) alone will save them from an excruciating headache and additional unbearable heartache. Imagine trying to fill out a mountain of paperwork – with limited information - while you're grieving. Be sure they have the phone number and/or a local office contact for Veteran's Affairs. Someone there will be more than happy to walk them through the process. A little tip: If you already have an online account with the Department of Veteran's Affairs, access to the information on the account will prove very helpful – especially if you're getting benefits (i.e., disability/pension/etc.). Be sure to share the details on how to access your account. Additionally, a copy of your military records – including the DD-214 form can be requested by visiting the National Archives site and selectin Request for Military Records.

Believe it or not, I do have a story to share! Think about this! After my friend lost her dad, we went to the funeral home to manage the arrangements. Thankfully, somewhere along the line an entire information packet had been given to her mom. If there was anything to be read, she'd give it to me to determine whether it had any significant information. Anyone who knows me knows that I read everything – so of course I read the entire packet. There was a brochure outlining different benefits – specifically a section for service arrangements and what is covered for a Veteran. I kept the brochure with me as a point of reference while we discussed the arrangements. Although we'd chosen a well-known company, apparently the funeral director at that location was rather inexperienced in how to properly handle the final arrangements for Veterans. This was amusing considering he had just given us a wonderful speech about how much they value working with the families of our Veterans.

They were going to charge us for services that are listed as covered benefits for Veterans! When I pointed this out, he said he wasn't familiar and asked where I'd gotten my information. I told him it was in the handy brochure I was holding. I happily pointed to the line on the brochure. He said he'd have to call his supervisor to discuss it. When he returned, he acknowledged that I was correct and that certain charges were covered; however, the Department of Veteran's Affairs reimburses you for the covered expenses vs the funeral home either crediting or not charging for the covered item/service. That was not in the brochure – oops.

Imagine that! Did you know that? We sure didn't! I stand corrected.

Did you know that unlike civilian life insurance, your Veteran's life insurance benefit does not pay out to the funeral home? They pay your beneficiary directly and your beneficiary is responsible for paying the funeral home. So, there's no "Hey, here's the life insurance company, policy number, and amount, let's plan a funeral." The conversation goes more like, "Now that we've planned the funeral, here's how much it'll cost you and how do you plan to pay?" So, we left there with a service contract, a bill, and another form on the list to fill out – the Application for Burial Benefits. I tell you, that form DD-214 really was a lifesaver!

We were able to call to file the claim for life insurance benefits. It seemed super simple during the call and just when we were about to say that was easy, we were referred to, you guessed it – another form.

We ended up filling out what seemed like a never-ending packet of forms. We did a lot of guessing about which sections to complete and which sections to skip. We weren't one hundred percent sure which sections were or were not applicable. Just when we thought we were finished, some of the forms required the signature of two witnesses! Who knew?!

Well, as you can see, the gift of knowledge is even more critical as a Veteran because - in order to access the benefits related to your much appreciated service - there's a vast amount of paperwork and information that your loved ones will need to know about and understand to manage the process as they manage the heartache of losing you.

CERTIFICATE OF RELEASE OR DISCHARGE FROM ACTIVE DUTY

This Report Contains Information Subject to the Privacy Act of 1974, As Amended.

OMB No. 0704-0188
OMB approval expires 2027/02/28

1. NAME *(Last, First, Middle)*	2. DEPARTMENT, COMPONENT AND BRANCH	3. SOCIAL SECURITY NUMBER
JOHNSON, MICHAEL ANDREW	ARMY/RA	123-45-6789

4a. GRADE, RATE OR RANK	4b. PAY GRADE	5. DATE OF BIRTH *(YYYYMMDD)*	6. RESERVE OBLIGATION TERMINATION DATE *(YYYYMMDD)*
SGT	E-5	19920115	20300114

7a. PLACE OF ENTRY INTO ACTIVE DUTY	7b. HOME OF RECORD AT TIME OF ENTRY *(City and state, or complete address if known)*
AUSTIN, TX	DALLAS, TX

8a. LAST DUTY ASSIGNMENT AND MAJOR COMMAND	8b. STATION WHERE SEPARATED
B CO, 1-23 INFANTRY REGIMENT, 2ND INFANTRY BRIGADE COMBAT TEAM, 4TH INFANTRY DIVISION, FORT CARSON, CO	FORT CARSON, CO

9. COMMAND TO WHICH TRANSFERRED	10. SGLI COVERAGE	11. PRIMARY SPECIALTY *(List number, title and years and months in specialty. List additional specialty numbers and titles involving periods of one or more years.)*
US ARMY TRANSITION COMMAND	NONE	11B10, INFANTRYMAN, 6 YEARS, 2 MONTHS

12. RECORD OF SERVICE

a. DATE ENTERED AD THIS PERIOD	20180515
b. SEPARATION DATE THIS PERIOD	20240514
c. NET ACTIVE SERVICE THIS PERIOD	6 YEARS, 0 MONTHS, 0 DAYS
d. TOTAL PRIOR ACTIVE SERVICE	0 YEARS, 0 MONTHS, 0 DAYS
e. TOTAL PRIOR INACTIVE SERVICE	0 YEARS, 0 MONTHS, 0 DAYS
f. FOREIGN SERVICE	1 YEAR, 2 MONTHS, 15 DAYS
g. SEA SERVICE	0 YEARS, 0 MONTHS, 0 DAYS
h. INITIAL ENTRY TRAINING	ONE STATION UNIT TRAINING

13. DECORATIONS, MEDALS, BADGES, CITATIONS AND CAMPAIGN RIBBONS AWARDED OR AUTHORIZED

ARMY COMMENDATION MEDAL
ARMY ACHIEVEMENT MEDAL
NATIONAL DEFENSE SERVICE MEDAL
GLOBAL WAR ON TERRORISM SERVICE MEDAL
ARMY SERVICE RIBBON
OVERSEAS SERVICE RIBBON
COMBAT INFANTRYMAN BADGE
MARKSMANSHIP QUALIFICATION BADGE (RIFLE)
DRIVER AND MECHANIC BADGE

14. MILITARY EDUCATION *(Course title, number of weeks, and month and year completed)*

INFANTRYMAN ONE STATION UNIT TRAINING, 14 WEEKS, AUG 2018
COMBATIVE SKILLS TRAINER, 2 WEEKS, MAR 2021

15a. COMMISSIONED THROUGH SERVICE ACADEMY	15b. COMMISSIONED THROUGH ROTC SCHOLARSHIP	15c. ENLISTED UNDER LOAN REPAYMENT PROGRAM
NO	NO	NO

16. DAYS ACCRUED LEAVE PAID	17. MEMBER WAS PROVIDED COMPLETE DENTAL EXAMINATION AND ALL APPROPRIATE DENTAL SERVICES AND TREATMENT	18. REMARKS
30	YES	NONE

19a. MAILING ADDRESS AFTER SEPARATION *(Include ZIP Code)*	19b. NEAREST RELATIVE *(Name and address - include ZIP Code)*
1234 OAK HILL DRIVE DALLAS, TX 75201	SARAH JOHNSON (SPOUSE) 1234 OAK HILL DRIVE DALLAS, TX 75201

20. MEMBER REQUESTS COPY 6 BE SENT TO *(Specify state/locality)*
TEXAS

21. SIGNATURE OF MEMBER BEING SEPARATED	22. OFFICIAL AUTHORIZED TO SIGN *(Typed name, grade and title)*	23. SIGNATURE OF OFFICIAL AUTHORIZED TO SIGN	24. DATE *(YYYYMMDD)*
Michael A. Johnson	T. R. WILLIAMS, LTC COMMANDING	*T. R. Williams*	20240514

25. SEPARATION AUTHORITY	26. SEPARATION CODE	27. REENTRY CODE	28. NARRATIVE REASON FOR SEPARATION
AR 635-200, CHAPTER 4	KFF	1	COMPLETION OF REQUIRED ACTIVE SERVICE

29. DATES OF TIME LOST DURING THIS PERIOD	30. MEMBER REQUESTS COPY 3 BE SENT TO THE CENTRAL OFFICE OF THE DEPARTMENT OF VETERANS AFFAIRS	31. SERVICE CHARACTERIZATION
NONE	YES	HONORABLE

DD FORM 214, AUG 2020 PREVIOUS EDITIONS ARE OBSOLETE. MEMBER - 4

All documents and military records depicted are fictional recreations created for illustrative purposes only.

Chapter 6:

So, Write a Love Letter

Where is your life insurance policy? Where is your will? Who knows about it? Did you give a copy of these documents to your executor/executrix? Does your attorney have a copy on file for you? Does anyone know who your attorney is? It is extremely difficult losing the family member who handled all of the day-to-day finances and administrative planning in the home. I remember receiving a call from a distraught, confused widow when I worked in a call center.

She didn't know anything about the household finances or where to find the documents to help her figure it out. How did she know where to call? Great question! She was now responsible for reading the mail. She received more than condolence letters; she received past due notices for outstanding loans. Talk about an unwelcome visitor! She had to learn to navigate the financials while grieving the loss of her husband because he never shared any information with her. She also learned that the bank account that he had been using to pay the bills had no beneficiary listed. As a result, she had no access to the funds in the account as the bank had frozen them subject to the outcome of probate. She was dumbfounded. How could her husband overlook adding a beneficiary to his bank account?

Do you remember me sharing my uncle's end-of-life experience? Would you believe that about five minutes after he was pronounced, a hospital representative began asking me what seemed to be very cold but necessary questions (age, date of birth, next of kin, who will handle the body, etc.). I knew most of the answers, although I was not prepared for this part of the process. Worse yet, I had to find my aunt – his wife - to help fill in the blanks. What's so bad about that? you ask. I first had to tell her he had taken his last breath – and ask her to answer the questions that I could not.

In order to avoid this situation, in addition to your estate planning documents, put together a letter of intentions package. Providing instructions and information about you that they will need in order to successfully manage your affairs should help reduce the level of stress your loved ones will experience during this process.

What should you do now? This section is designed to share information with you to better prepare so that you and/or your loved ones don't end up in the comedy of errors that were shared with you in this book.

I don't purport to have all of the answers, as estate planning has many facets and moving parts – far too many to note here. This book is designed to get you to move beyond thinking about the importance of estate planning to actually preparing your estate plan. There is a phrase out there that says, "Be the source of the source, not the source." This applies here because each state has different laws related to estate planning. The last thing I would want to do is mislead you. I recommend you consult a local attorney for your state. If you don't already have someone in mind, I've provided the links for each state's bar association as a resource to help you locate and connect with someone in your area.

It is true, you can prepare a will on your own. Again, because there are many moving parts to estate planning, especially if you have children, a business, multiple properties, a spouse, children from a previous marriage, etc., it's important that you seek assistance from a professional.

Don't be among the 43% of Americans who fail to plan simply because they just haven't gotten around to it.v Love your loved ones enough to leave them with instructions to follow on your behalf. Save them from the unnecessary pain of what happens when you die … for real!

SAMPLE LETTER OF INTENT

Letter of Intent for Final Planning

Please use this Letter of Intent as a guide to manage my final arrangements, distribute assets, and other important matters. This letter is a supplement to my will and other estate planning documents.

1. Information

- Full Name: [Your full legal name]
- Date of Birth: [Your date of birth]
- Social Security Number: [Last 4 digits: XXX-XX-]
- Executor: [Name and contact information of executor/trustee]
- Key Contacts:
    - Attorney: [Name, firm, phone, email]
    - Financial Advisor: [Name, firm, phone, email]
    - Insurance Agent: [Name, phone, email]

2. Final Arrangements

- Funeral Preferences:
    - Burial/Cremation preference
    - Location: (cemetery or crematory name, city/state)
    - Type of service: (religious, military, memorial, etc.)

- Specific requests: (e.g., music, readings, or flowers)

- Obituary:
  - I would like my obituary published in (list specific newspapers/ online platforms)
  - Key details to include: (career, accomplishments, family members, hobbies, etc.)
- Memorial Donations:
  - In lieu of flowers, please direct donations to: List charity or organization

3. Financial Instructions

- Accounts and Financial Information:
  - List bank name(s) and account types (checking, savings)
  - List of recurring bills (utilities, subscriptions, etc.)
- Debts and Liabilities:
  - Ensure that the following debts are resolved: List debts
  - Contact creditors and notify them of my passing.

4. Distribution of Personal Items

- I have specified most asset distributions in my will; however, I would like to address the following personal items:
  - Item and Recipient

- Item and Recipient

5. Digital and Online Accounts

- I have documented my digital accounts and passwords in (list location of record, e.g., password manager or safe)
- Please ensure the following accounts are handled accordingly:
    - Social media, email (list and give instructions to close)

6. Additional Instructions

- Pets:
    - Please ensure the care of (list pets)
    - Contact (list name of person who'll care for your pet)

7. Location of Important Documents

The following documents are stored in (list location):

- Will and trust documents
- Birth and marriage certificates
- Insurance policies
- Deeds, titles, and other property documents
- Tax returns and financial records

Closing Note:

I hope this letter will provide clarity and comfort during such a difficult time. Please know that I am at peace with these decisions and eternally grateful for your love and support.

- If you want to write a special note to your family, use this space to do so.

Your Signature

The content provided is for informational purposes only and should not be considered legal advice. For personalized assistance or verification of legal compliance in your jurisdiction, consult with an attorney or estate planning professional.

HELPFUL RESOURCES

This section is designed to provide helpful information and/or resources to make this process a little easier to navigate when the time comes.

Links:
Help Writing an Obituary: www.Legacy.com ; www.ObitKit.com

Help Starting the Conversation of Your End-of-Life Wishes: http://theconversationproject.org/wp-content/uploads/2020/12/ConversationStarterGuide.pdf

Department of Veteran's Affairs: www.VA.gov

National Archives: https://www.archives.gov/veterans/military-service-records

Office of Survivors Assistance: https://www.va.gov/survivors/

LIFE INSURANCE POLICY COMPARISON SHEET-WHOLE LIFE

	Name of Insurance Company:
Features:	Policy 1
Insurance Type (Term/Whole/Universal/Variable)	
Amount of Coverage	
Policy Term	
Premium (monthly/quarterly/annually)	
Cash Value (Yes/No)	
Child/Spouse Rider	
Accelerated Death Benefit (Yes/No; Details)	
Waiver of Premium (Yes/No; Details)	
Accidental Death Benefit (Yes/No; Details)	
Flexibility (Yes/No; Details)	
Exclusions (Details)	
Company Reputation (Excellent/Good/Fair)	
Customer Service (Excellent/Good/Fair)	

Name of Insurance Company:	Name of Insurance Company:
Policy 2	Policy 3

LIFE INSURANCE POLICY COMPARISON SHEET-TERM LIFE

	Name of Insurance Company:
Features:	Policy 1
Insurance Type (Term/ Whole/Universal/ Variable)	
Amount of Coverage	
Policy Term	
Premium (monthly/ quarterly/annually)	
Cash Value (Yes/No)	
Child/Spouse Rider	
Accelerated Death Benefit (Yes/No; Details)	
Waiver of Premium (Yes/No; Details)	
Accidental Death Benefit (Yes/No; Details)	
Flexibility (Yes/No; Details)	
Exclusions (Details)	
Company Reputation (Excellent/Good/Fair)	
Customer Service (Excellent/Good/Fair)	

Name of Insurance Company:	**Name of Insurance Company:**
Policy 2	Policy 3

LIFE INSURANCE POLICY COMPARISON SHEET- UNIVERSAL LIFE

	Name of Insurance Company:
Features:	Policy 1
Insurance Type (Term/ Whole/Universal/ Variable)	
Amount of Coverage	
Policy Term	
Premium (monthly/ quarterly/annually)	
Cash Value (Yes/No)	
Child/Spouse Rider	
Accelerated Death Benefit (Yes/No; Details)	
Waiver of Premium (Yes/No; Details)	
Accidental Death Benefit (Yes/No; Details)	
Flexibility (Yes/No; Details)	
Exclusions (Details)	
Company Reputation (Excellent/Good/Fair)	
Customer Service (Excellent/Good/Fair)	

Name of Insurance Company:	**Name of Insurance Company:**
Policy 2	Policy 3

LIFE INSURANCE POLICY COMPARISON SHEET-VARIABLE LIFE

	Name of Insurance Company:
Features:	Policy 1
Insurance Type (Term/ Whole/Universal/ Variable)	
Amount of Coverage	
Policy Term	
Premium (monthly/ quarterly/annually)	
Cash Value (Yes/No)	
Child/Spouse Rider	
Accelerated Death Benefit (Yes/No; Details)	
Waiver of Premium (Yes/No; Details)	
Accidental Death Benefit (Yes/No; Details)	
Flexibility (Yes/No; Details)	
Exclusions (Details)	
Company Reputation (Excellent/Good/Fair)	
Customer Service (Excellent/Good/Fair)	

Name of Insurance Company:	**Name of Insurance Company:**
Policy 2	Policy 3

GLOSSARY OF TERMS

1. **Advance Directive:** A document outlining your healthcare preferences, such as life support, if you can't make decisions for yourself.
2. **Administrator:** A person appointed by the court to manage an estate if someone dies without a will.
3. **Beneficiary:** A person or organization who receives assets or benefits from a will, trust, transfer/pay on death account, or insurance policy.
4. **Burial:** Placing a deceased person's body in the ground, usually in a casket.
5. **Burial Allowance:** Financial assistance from the VA to help cover burial or funeral costs for a Veteran.
6. **Burial Flag:** A U.S. flag provided by the VA to honor a Veteran during their funeral, typically draped over the casket or displayed with the urn.
7. **Casket:** A box used to hold a body for burial or cremation.
8. **Charitable Trust:** A trust that gives money or property to a charity, often with tax benefits.

9. **Codicil:** An amendment to a will that makes changes without rewriting the entire document.
10. **Columbarium:** A structure with small spaces (niches) to hold urns containing cremated remains.
11. **Committal Service:** A brief graveside ceremony, often in a cemetery, to honor the deceased before burial or placement in a columbarium.
12. **Cremation:** The process of turning a body into ashes through high heat.
13. **Death Certificate:** An official document that records the cause, date, and place of someone's death.
14. **Deed:** A legal document transferring ownership of property.
15. **Direct Burial:** A burial without a ceremony or viewing beforehand.
16. **Direct Cremation:** A cremation without a ceremony or viewing beforehand.
17. **Digital Assets:** Online property like social media accounts, email, or cryptocurrencies, included in an estate plan.
18. **Durable Power of Attorney:** A legal document that lets someone handle your financial or legal affairs, even if you become incapacitated.

19. **Eulogy:** A speech given at a funeral or memorial service to honor and remember the deceased.
20. **Estate:** Everything a person owns at the time of their death, including property, money, and belongings.
21. **Estate Tax:** A tax on the value of a person's estate after they die, levied by the government.
22. **Executor:** The person named in a will to manage the estate and carry out the deceased's instructions.
23. **Final Resting Place:** The location where a body or ashes are laid to rest, such as a grave or columbarium.
24. **Funeral Home:** A business that provides services for the deceased, including preparing the body and hosting services.
25. **Funeral Honors Coordinator:** A person who helps arrange military honors for a deceased Veteran.
26. **Gift Tax:** A tax on large gifts given during someone's lifetime above certain limits.
27. **Grantor (or Settlor):** The person who creates a trust.
28. **Green Burial:** An eco-friendly burial without embalming, using biodegradable materials.

29. **Guardianship:** A legal arrangement where someone is assigned to care for a minor child or incapacitated adult.
30. **Healthcare Proxy:** A document that lets someone make medical decisions for you if you're unable to.
31. **Heir:** A person entitled to inherit from someone who dies without a will.
32. **Honorary Pallbearer:** A person recognized for their connection to the deceased but who doesn't carry the casket.
33. **Interment:** The act of placing a body or ashes in the ground or a mausoleum.
34. **Intestate:** When someone dies without a will, and state laws decide how their assets are distributed.
35. **Irrevocable Trust:** A trust that cannot be changed or canceled after it's created.
36. **Letters Testamentary:** A court-issued document giving an executor the authority to manage the deceased's estate.
37. **Living Trust (or Revocable Trust):** A trust created during a person's lifetime to manage their assets and distribute them after death. It can be changed or canceled anytime.
38. **Living Will:** A document specifying your medical care preferences if you cannot communicate them.

39. **Marital Deduction:** A tax rule allowing spouses to transfer unlimited assets to each other without taxes.
40. **Mausoleum:** A building where caskets or urns are placed instead of being buried in the ground.
41. **Medallion:** A metal emblem provided by the VA for Veterans buried in private cemeteries, used instead of a government headstone.
42. **Memorial Donations:** Donations made to a charity in honor of the deceased instead of sending flowers.
43. **Memorial Service:** A ceremony honoring the deceased, usually without the body present.
44. **Military Funeral Honors:** A ceremony for Veterans that includes a flag presentation, playing of "Taps," and possibly a rifle salute.
45. **Outer Burial Container (Vault or Liner):** A protective container placed around the casket in the ground to prevent the grave from collapsing.
46. **Pallbearer:** A person who helps carry the casket during the funeral.
47. **Pour-Over Will:** A will that transfers any remaining property into a trust after someone dies.
48. **Power of Attorney (POA):** A legal document giving someone authority to act on your behalf for specific tasks.

49. **Presidential Memorial Certificate:** A certificate signed by the U.S. President to honor the service of a deceased Veteran.

50. **Prepaid Funeral Plan:** A plan where funeral costs are paid in advance.

51. **Preplanning (or Prearrangements):** Making funeral and burial decisions ahead of time to ease the burden on loved ones.

52. **Probate:** The legal process of validating a will, paying debts, and distributing assets.

53. **Repatriation:** Returning a deceased person's body or ashes to their home country or another location.

54. **Rifle Salute:** A ceremonial firing of rifles performed as a sign of respect during a Veteran's funeral.

55. **Scattering:** Releasing ashes in a meaningful location, such as a garden or body of water.

56. **Service-Connected Death Benefits:** Additional VA benefits provided if a Veteran's death is related to their military service.

57. **Spouse and Dependent Eligibility:** A Veteran's spouse or children may qualify for burial in a national cemetery.

58. **Survivor Benefits:** Ongoing support or payments to a Veteran's family after their death.

59. **Taps:** A bugle call played at military funerals to honor the deceased Veteran.
60. **Testamentary Trust:** A trust created in a will that takes effect after the person's death.
61. **Trust:** An arrangement where a trustee manages assets for the benefit of others.
62. **Trustee:** The person or organization managing a trust.
63. **Urn:** A container used to hold cremated remains.
64. **VA (Veteran's Affairs):** A government agency providing benefits and services to Veterans and their families.
65. **VA Burial Benefits:** Benefits provided by the VA, like burial in a national cemetery or a free grave marker.
66. **Viewing (or Visitation):** A time for family and friends to see the deceased, say goodbye, and offer condolences.
67. **Will:** A document that states who gets your property and who will care for minor children after your death.

End Notes

i 2024 Insurance Barometer Study, Life Happens and LIMRA https://www.limra.com/siteassets/research/research- abstracts-shared/2024/securing-the-future/2024-insurance-barometer---securing-the-future-infographic.pdf

ii Caring.Com 2024 Will and Living Trust Survey https://www.caring.com/caregivers/estate-planning/wills-survey/

iii The Conversation Project National Survey, 2018 https://theconversationproject.org/wp- content/uploads/2018/06/TCP_OnePager.pdf

iv Hospice News, 2023 Jim Parker https://hospicenews.com/2023/04/12/only-22-of-americans-have-documented- end-of-life-wishes/

v Caring.Com 2024 Will and Living Trust Survey https://www.caring.com/caregivers/estate-planning/wills-survey/

Your journey doesn't end here.

Visit **www.AffairsInOrderNOW.com**
for additional resources, tools, and information
to help you every step of the way.

Simply scan the QR code below to get started.

Notes

Notes

Notes

About the Author

Leneiva Head, J.D., is a lawyer and the Principal Broker/Owner of Welcome Home Realty™, a Nashville-based real estate firm she opened more than 17 years ago. A native Nashvillian, she has spent more than 25 years helping individuals and families navigate some of life's most important transitions. Her work and expertise have been featured in publications and media outlets including *Forbes*, Cheddar, and *Reader's Digest*.

Throughout her 25-year career in real estate and risk management, Leneiva has worked closely with families facing major life events, including homeownership, financial planning, caregiving responsibilities, and the loss of loved ones. Through those experiences, she witnessed firsthand the difference preparation can make—and the challenges families face when important affairs have not been organized in advance. Over the years, she found herself helping grieving families navigate the paperwork, decisions, responsibilities, and unexpected obstacles that often follow the death of a loved one.

Long after the real estate and insurance transactions ended, she continued to answer questions, locate resources, explain processes, and help people work through situations they never expected to face. She did so simply because someone needed help. These experiences revealed a common theme: many families were left trying to make important decisions during one of the most difficult seasons of their lives without a clear roadmap to follow. That realization inspired her to write *What Happens When You Die...For Real?*

Drawing from decades of professional experience and countless conversations with families in transition, Leneiva is passionate about helping people prepare today so their loved ones can experience greater clarity, confidence, and peace of mind tomorrow. Her mission is simple: helping families get their affairs in order—NOW.